For the Birds.

With all my Love

Brenda

Sept 11th

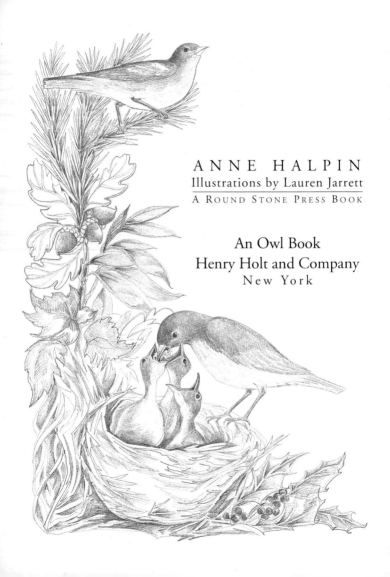

ANNE HALPIN

Illustrations by Lauren Jarrett

A ROUND STONE PRESS BOOK

An Owl Book
Henry Holt and Company
New York

THE NATIONAL WILDLIFE FEDERATION

For the Birds!

A Handy Guide to Attracting Birds to Your Backyard

Henry Holt and Company, Inc.
Publishers since 1866
115 West 18th Street
New York, New York 10011

Henry Holt ® is a registered trademark
of Henry Holt and Company, Inc.

Published in Canada by Fitzhenry & Whiteside Ltd.,
195 Allstate Parkway, Markham, Ontario L3R 4T8.

Library of Congress Cataloging-in-Publication Data
Halpin, Anne Moyer.
For the birds: a handy guide to attracting birds
to your backyard/by Anne Halpin.—1st ed.
p.   cm.
Includes index
1. Bird attracting.   2. Gardening to attract birds.   3. Birds—
Feeding and feeds.   I. National Wildlife Federation.   II. Title.
QL676.5.H32   1996   95-36868
598'.07234—dc20   CIP

ISBN 0-8050-4064-1 (An Owl Book: pbk)

Henry Holt books are available for special promotions and premiums.
For details contact: Director, Special Markets.

First edition—1996

A ROUND STONE PRESS BOOK
Directors: Marsha Melnick, Susan E. Meyer, Paul Fargis
Developmental Editor: Nick Viorst
Designer: Bonni Leon-Berman

Printed in Hong Kong
All first editions are printed on acid-free paper. ∞

10 9 8 7 6 5 4 3 2 1

Contents

A Word from the NWF

When I was growing up, my family's garden had vegetables, gladiolas, calendulas, zinnias, and shrubs. A row of forsythia screened our front yard to the east. Azaleas, hollies, yews, and junipers framed the house, creating a green oasis even as the surrounding grass browned out in the summer's heat. Above these loomed trees: glorious American hollies, flowering dogwoods, a short-lived but much-climbed-upon weeping willow, and sturdy, aromatic pitch pines.

These plants weren't static denizens of the yard, but, rather, vital providers of food and shelter to flocks of evening grosbeaks, American goldfinches, robins, cardinals, chickadees, downy woodpeckers, and titmice. Supplemented by feeders, birdbaths, and nesting boxes, the trees, shrubs, and flowers created a haven for birds, which in turn enlivened my childhood days with their song, movement, color, and drama.

Tens of millions of people in North America brighten their lives by providing for the needs of birds, offering food from various plants and feeders, clean water, safe areas to escape marauding house cats or summer squalls,

and secure cover in which to construct nests. They are repaid many times over in the entertainment, many wonderful learning opportunities,
and beauty their visitors bring to the garden.

But this bird-wise activity is also valuable on another level beyond the pleasure it brings. For if birds are to settle into or even visit a neighborhood, they must have these essentials. Indeed, sometimes an inviting backyard can mean the difference between an increasing resident bird population and local extinction. Or between a successful and an unsuccessful northward migration by thrushes, warblers, and vireos.

This book can teach you the basics of attracting birds to your property, through actions big and small, whether you live on a vast rural estate or in a terraced city apartment. Equally important, the book can help you help our wild birds continue to be a vibrant, dynamic part of the world in which we and they are partners.

Craig Tufts,
Chief Naturalist and Manager,
Backyard Wildlife Habitat Program,
National Wildlife Federation

Introduction

Birds are magical creatures. These sprites of the air delight us with their colorful plumage, their lilting songs, and their comical antics at feeders. In all their diversity birds are undeniably fascinating creatures.

Of all the wild creatures with whom we share our planet, birds are perhaps the easiest to get to know. They are everywhere around us—in the country and the city, in fields and forests, prairies and deserts, in the mountains and by the sea. As they fly across the sky, flutter down to rest on tree branches and telephone wires, and call to each other across neighborhoods and open spaces, birds bring color and music to our world. Their songs enchant us and remind us of our links to the rest of the natural world. It's wonderful to wake up to the sounds of birds, and great fun to watch them as they go about the business of their lives. Watching birds around a backyard feeder or out in the wild can quickly become an absorbing activity.

Homeowners and gardeners can help nurture the feathered creatures that brighten our world, even if only on a modest level. We can become sensitive to the needs of wild birds, and provide habitat areas and sources of nourishment for them in our backyards. In becoming more involved with birds we earn for ourselves the bonus of a richly rewarding hobby and a source of endless entertainment and education.

This book is an introduction to things you can do to attract birds right into your own backyard. No matter where you live, you can make your yard an inviting site for all kinds of birds. And doing so doesn't cost a lot of money, or take a lot of time.

If you like to garden, you'll find a range of particularly useful suggestions for turning your yard into a haven for birds—by adding plants that provide them with much-appreciated food and shelter. Many of these ideas are simple enough even to appeal to those not generally inclined to gardening. You will also learn about different kinds of feeders you can install and what to put in them, birdbaths and other water sources that will draw birds, and nesting boxes and nesting shelves to put up. You will even find some tips on enjoying the birds that will come to visit (and even stay) in your backyard.

And whether you decide to adopt many of the suggestions in the following pages or just one or two, you are certain to find the effort well rewarded.

Bird Essentials

The seemingly endless variety of birds that populate our planet make their homes in an extraordinary range of habitats. Some birds reside in fields, meadows, and prairies. Others dwell in the desert. Some birds live at the seashore amid beaches and dunes, near lakes, ponds, or streams, or in salt- or freshwater wetlands and waterways, hunting for fish, crabs, mollusks, and other seafood.

Many birds inhabit woodlands and forests, nesting in trees and dining on insects as well as berries and seeds. A few birds have adapted to the mowed lawns of suburbia or the developed spaces of towns and cities, contenting themselves with such trees and shrubs as can be found in backyards, parkland, and vacant lots. Some even tuck their nests into protected ledges of skyscrapers, high above the ground.

But no matter where birds live, and no matter what species they are, all share common needs. They need sources of food for both adults and young, water for drinking and cleaning themselves, and cover in which to escape predators and take shelter from bad weather. They also need protected places in which to build nests and raise their young.

There is considerable diversity in the types of foods the many different species of birds will eat. Fruit, seeds, nuts, and other plant products (such as pine cones, tree sap, and flower nectar) are the favored foods of quite a few birds. Lots of birds eat insects (including grubs) and caterpillars, and feed their young on them, too. They pick insects off leaves and stems, or catch them in flight, and dig worms and grubs out of the ground. Some birds have a variable diet, consuming insects in spring and summer, for themselves and their young, but eating other foods at other times of the year.

Water is also an essential part of a habitat for birds. They need a constant supply of fresh, clean water at all times of year, for both drinking and bathing. They also use water to moisten food they bring back to the nest for their young. Ponds, streams, pools, puddles, birdbaths, and even leaves on which rain or dew has collected all serve as water sources for birds. Some birds even eat snow.

Birds need cover to hide from predators, for protection from the elements, to nest, and to sleep at night. Birds find cover in a wide variety of places—evergreen and deciduous trees and shrubs, hedges, vines, bramble thickets, brush piles, cavities in tree trunks, the layer of dry leaves and twigs on the floor of a forest, in tall grass, in meadows and fields, rock ledges, under the eaves of buildings, and in nesting boxes.

The more of these essentials your yard provides, the more it becomes a haven for birds. And whether you already have a lush landscape or a simple city terrace, there are dozens of things you can do to provide what the birds want. You can make a few basic adjustments, putting up a couple of feeders and a birdbath, or you can go so far as to plan your entire home landscape around the needs of birds. It all depends on your own temperament and what you wish to accomplish.

Gardening for Birds

There is probably nothing more inviting to birds than a landscape featuring plants that provide them with food and cover. Whether it be a rich habitat of lush, fruit-bearing trees, shrubs, and vines, or simply a patch of seed-producing flowers and tall grasses, birds are naturally drawn to the right kinds of plants. By integrating these plants into your own garden, you can create an appealing, comfortable environment that birds will visit again and again. And especially if you start simple, you don't need to be a serious gardener to provide plants for birds.

By no means do plantings rule out your offering other forms of food and shelter for birds. They will still welcome a few feeders and nesting boxes to complement the plants. It just makes the yard even more attractive to them. And, of course, it is always a good idea to have a water source on the property.

What to plant

Food plants for birds are those that supply berries or other fruit, seeds, and nuts. Various trees and shrubs can provide these foods, and many trees provide sap, another source of nourishment for some birds. Cherries; crabapples, and hawthorns are all popular trees for birds, as are birches and cedars with their seed-filled cones. Shrubs like raspberry and blackberry brambles and sumac are good suppliers of food as well. And trees and shrubs are valuable food plants for another reason: they are the principal sources of insects that almost all birds eat, making them doubly alluring and the mainstays of any garden for birds.

Some easy-to-grow vines, such as wild grapes, and ground covers can also provide berries or small berrylike fruits that are good sources of food for birds. Grasses and wild-flowers, including thistles, goldenrod, and black-eyed Susans, are among the best seed sources. And flowers such as bee balm, coneflower, and fuchsia offer the nectar that some birds (notably hummingbirds) like to sip; these make up another important component of a bird garden.

Plants used as cover, to be service-able, should be bushy and at least 3 or 4 feet high. Birds will use deciduous and evergreen trees, shrubs, and vines for cover. Where winters are cold, evergreens are essential. To a large degree, the same plants that provide food make perfect cover plants. A grove of hollies, junipers, or oaks, for example, will meet both needs for a variety of birds. But you need not limit your choices to such multipurpose plants. If you have the space, you can put in some plants—such as maple, pines, and prickly pears—purely to provide shelter.

Don't overlook vines when considering plants for shelter, especially if they are also a food source. A wall thickly covered with ivy or Virginia creeper, or trumpet creeper growing in a leafy blanket over shrubs or a fence, provides excellent hiding places for many small birds. If there's a big tree stump or rock pile in your landscape, instead of removing it you could train a twining or tendrilled vine like trumpet honeysuckle to grow up and over it—and birds will take shelter there. Clinging vines will climb right up a stone wall without assistance from the gardener. A

Start your gardening for birds by observing the birds that already visit your yard, or your neighbors' properties, and also learn which birds are year-round residents or migratory visitors to your part of the country. When you know a bit about the kinds of birds that are likely to be in the area, you can learn which food and cover plants they like and provide accordingly. You can grow plants that appeal to the whole range of birds, or plant selectively to attract only your favorites.

meadow of grasses and wildflowers, or even a swath of lawn left unmowed will protect birds as well.

Obviously, if your property is small, you won't be able to provide all these types of plants. And even if you have a sizeable yard, you may not want to do so. Still, when it comes to attracting birds, even a few scattered plants can make a real difference.

Plants native to your region are especially good choices for bird gardens, because the birds are familiar with them and accustomed to the food and shelter they provide. This doesn't mean you must plant only native plants, but do include at least some. Then you will be sure of offering just what the birds will like.

How to plant

Although you certainly don't need to overhaul your yard completely to introduce plantings, ideally a garden for birds should be arranged to contain several types of plants of varying heights that together create layers of vegetation. There should be some large, tall trees such as oaks, maples, or beeches, and smaller understory trees like serviceberries and dogwoods, which can grow in the shade of the taller trees. The more natural and "wild-looking" the plantings, the better the birds will like it. Instead of planting individual trees or shrubs as ornamental specimens in the lawn, group them into hedgerows and borders, along with vines, flowers and grasses, and low ground covers. Make the borders at least 8 feet wide to provide a reasonable amount of food and cover. Let them curve and wind about the edges of the lawn.

In an out-of-the-way corner, let shrubs and vines grow into a dense thicket of greenery. Concentrate on planting fruit- and nut-bearing plants and letting them grow to their natural form. Prune them enough to prevent excessive branch-against-branch contact, and to remove dead and damaged growth, but no more. Neatly clipped topiaries won't do the trick.

If you need a more formal divider for a property line or to serve as a screen, plant an evergreen hedgerow of junipers, pines, hollies, or even a native rose species. Again, prune as little as possible—remember, you want the plants to produce fruit for birds to eat.

Plant flowers in informal mixed borders along with some shrubs and small trees, or consider a meadow planting of flowers and grasses in a sunny spot nearby.

Clearly, if you get into attracting birds in a serious way, you may need to change some of your ideas about gardening, and about how your yard should look. If you're creating a habitat for birds, you're simply more likely to have luck with a less manicured landscape. Instead of a neatly mowed lawn, you will find yourself planting a meadow, or just letting the grass grow into scrubby tangles in odd corners of the property. Instead of a neatly clipped hedge, a mixed hedgerow of shrubs and small trees will suit the birds better. Instead of roses and petunias you may find yourself planting wildflowers.

And whether you choose to incorporate elements of natural plantings into more traditional backyard settings or to transform your garden entirely, you will discover that the carefree, naturalistic plantings that birds prefer have a special untamed beauty of their own.

Trees and Shrubs

Trees and shrubs can provide food and shelter for birds of all kinds. The best selections for a bird garden are those that provide both. Here are a number of these trees and shrubs, along with listings of the birds that find them most appealing, and basic planting information.

Birches (*Betula* spp.) are fast-growing trees with cones that make good food sources for birds. Attractive to blue jays, cardinals, chickadees, finches, juncos, orioles, pine siskins, towhees, tufted titmice, vireos, and yellow-bellied sapsuckers. Plant in full sun to partial shade, and, in most cases, in moist soil—though some species, like grey or clump birches, prefer dry soil.

Blueberries (*Vaccinium* spp.) are shrubs that produce their blue fruits in summer. Attractive to bluebirds, blue jays, bobwhites, brown thrashers, cardinals, catbirds, cedar waxwings, flickers, hermit thrushes, mockingbirds, mourning doves, orioles, phoebes, scarlet tanagers, scrub jays, tufted titmice, white-throated sparrows, and woodpeckers (including yellow-bellied sapsuckers). Plant in full sun to partial shade, in moist, humusy, acidic soil.

Brambles (*Rubus* spp.) are trailing shrubs with thorny, drooping stems and toothed leaves. They supply raspberries or blackberries. Left unpruned, brambles form dense thickets. Attractive to brown thrashers, buntings, cardinals, catbirds, flickers, grosbeaks, jays, mockingbirds, mourning doves, orioles, phoebes, quail, robins, sparrows, tanagers, thrushes, towhees, warblers, waxwings, white-eyed vireos, and woodpeckers. Plant in full sun, in well-drained average soil.

Cherries (*Prunus* spp.), in edible, ornamental, and wild varieties, are trees that supply fruit for a number of birds. Attractive to bluebirds, blue jays, brown thrashers, cardinals, catbirds, cedar waxwings, evening grosbeaks, finches, flickers, mockingbirds, red-eyed vireos, robins, scarlet tanagers, sparrows, thrushes, towhees, and woodpeckers (including yellow-bellied sapsuckers). Plant in full sun to light shade, in moist but well-drained, humusy average soil.

Crab apples (*Malus* spp.) are small to medium deciduous trees with pink, red, or white flowers in spring. They produce small, round, red or yellow apples in late summer. Attractive to bluebirds, blue jays, bobwhites, cardinals, catbirds, cedar waxwings, finches, flickers, grosbeaks, mockingbirds, orioles, red-eyed vireos, robins, towhees, warblers, and yellow-bellied sapsuckers. Plant in full sun, in well-drained average soil.

Dogwoods (*Cornus* spp.) are small to medium deciduous trees or shrubs that have glossy green leaves, with white flowers in spring, colorful fall foliage, and clusters of red, white, or blue fruits in midsummer to fall. They are good understory trees. Attractive to bluebirds, bobwhites, brown thrashers, cardinals, catbirds, cedar waxwings, finches, flickers, grosbeaks, hermit thrushes, mockingbirds, phoebes, red-eyed vireos, robins, scarlet tanagers, sparrows, thrushes, towhees, and woodpeckers (including yellow-bellied sapsuckers). Plant in full sun to light shade, in moist but well-drained, humusy average soil.

Hawthorns (*Crataegus* spp.) are small, dense, spreading deciduous trees with thorny branches, white or pink flowers, and colorful autumn foliage. They produce red fruits. Attractive to blue jays, bobwhites, brown thrashers, buntings, cardinals, catbirds, evening grosbeaks, flickers, hummingbirds, mockingbirds, purple finches, robins, sparrows, and thrushes. Plant in full sun, average to poor soil of either acid or alkaline pH.

Hollies (*Ilex* spp.) are broad-leaved evergreen shrubs or small trees with thick, glossy leaves that are spiny in some species and have small red, black, or yellow berries on female plants in autumn and winter. Attractive to bluebirds, blue jays, bobwhites, brown thrashers, cardinals, catbirds, cedar waxwings, chickadees, flickers, mockingbirds, mourning doves, nuthatches, phoebes, robins, thrushes, towhees, tufted titmice, warblers, and yellow-bellied sapsuckers. Plant in full sun to partial shade (some species tolerate more shade), in most cases in well-drained average soil—although winterberries and other deciduous hollies prefer damp soil.

Junipers, cedars (*Juniperus* spp.) are treelike, bushy, or low and spreading coniferous evergreens, with green to blue-green foliage and berrylike female cones. Attractive to brown thrashers, cardinals, cedar waxwings, chipping sparrows, flickers, grosbeaks, juncos, mockingbirds, mourning doves, phoebes, purple finches, robins, scarlet tanagers, sparrows, thrushes, vireos, woodpeckers, and yellow-rumped warblers. Plant in full sun to partial shade, in well-drained average soil.

Mulberries (*Morus* spp.) are trees with red, white, or blue-black fruits that are good food for many birds. Attractive to blue jays, bobwhites, brown thrashers, catbirds, cedar waxwings, dark-eyed juncos, finches, flickers, grosbeaks, mockingbirds, northern orioles, robins, scarlet tanagers, song sparrows, towhees, tufted titmice, vireos, and wood thrushes. Plant in full sun, in any well-drained soil.

Oaks (*Quercus* spp.) are slow-growing trees that can be deciduous or evergreen, shrubby or tall. Most have lobed leaves and bear acorns in fall. Attractive to blue-gray gnatcatchers, bobwhites, brown thrashers, cardinals, Carolina wrens, flickers, jays, mourning doves, nuthatches, orioles, robins, rose-breasted grosbeaks, tanagers, towhees, tufted titmice, and yellow-bellied sapsuckers. Plant in full sun, in well-drained soil.

Serviceberries (*Amelanchier* spp.) are deciduous shrubs or small trees that produce berrylike dark fruit in summer. They are good understory trees. Attractive to bluebirds, brown thrashers, cardinals, catbirds, cedar waxwings, chickadees, dark-eyed juncos, flickers, goldfinches, grosbeaks, grouse, jays, mourning doves, orioles, phoebes, robins, song sparrows, tanagers, thrushes, mockingbirds, towhees, tufted titmice, turkeys, wood ducks, and woodpeckers (including yellow-bellied sapsuckers). Plant in full sun to partial shade, in well-drained soil with an acid pH.

Sumacs (*Rhus* spp.) are shrubs that provide berries that are food for many birds. Attractive to bluebirds, bluejays, brown thrashers, cardinals, catbirds, flickers, juncos, mockingbirds, mourning doves, phoebes, quail, robins, thrushes, towhees, and woodpeckers. Plant in full sun to partial shade, in any average soil. Sumacs are drought-tolerant.

Viburnums (*Viburnum* spp.) are deciduous or evergreen shrubs with dark fruits in late summer. Attractive to bluebirds, bobwhites, brown thrashers, cardinals, catbirds, cedar waxwings, flickers, hermit thrushes, mockingbirds, purple finches, robins, rose-breasted grosbeaks, and sparrows. Plant in full sun to partial shade, in moist but well-drained soil.

Wild roses (*Rosa* spp.) are shrubs that, after blooming, produce round, usually red, fruits called hips. Attractive to bobwhites, brown thrashers, buntings, cardinals, catbirds, dark-eyed juncos, evening grosbeaks, goldfinches, mockingbirds, robins, sparrows, towhees, thrushes, waxwings, and yellow warblers. Plant in full sun, in well-drained average to fertile soil.

If you have plenty of room in your garden, feel free to add some trees and shrubs that serve exclusively as cover plants for birds. Good choices for a range of climates include elms (*Ulmus* spp.), maples (*Acer* spp.), and pines (*Pinus* spp.). In warm, dry climates, you can try prickly pears (*Opuntia* spp.), a species of cactus with oval pads covered with spines or bristles that produce lovely yellow flowers in spring or summer. In cooler climates, spruces (*Picea* spp.) are a fine option.

Vines and Ground Covers

Many vines (as well as shrubs that behave like vines) and ground covers provide birds with both food and shelter. Here are a few good selections for your bird garden.

Firethorns (*Pyracantha* spp.) are shrubs with long, trailing branches and bright orange-to-red berries that can be treated like vines—allowed to ramble over the ground or trained to climb a trellis against a wall. Attractive to blue jays, brown thrashers, cardinals, catbirds, cedar waxwings, hermit thrushes, mockingbirds, purple finches, robins, song sparrows, and wood thrushes. Plant in full sun, in well-drained, acid soil.

Grapes (*Vitis* spp.) are vines with clusters of green, purple-red, or deep purple fruit ripening in late summer. Attractive to bluebirds, blue jays, bobwhites, brown thrashers, cardinals, catbirds, cedar waxwings, flickers, grosbeaks, mockingbirds, mourning doves, orioles, red-eyed vireos, scarlet tanagers, towhees, thrushes, tufted titmice, and woodpeckers (including yellow-bellied sapsuckers). Plant in full sun, in well-drained, fertile soil.

Honeysuckle (*Lonicera* spp.) may take the form of shrubs or vines, depending on the species. They have more or less oval leaves, and white, yellow, pink, or orange flowers, and red or black honeysuckle fruits. They grow dense and tangled when left unpruned. Invasive Japanese honeysuckles should be avoided. Attractive to bluebirds, brown thrashers, catbirds, cedar waxwings, dark-eyed juncos, evening grosbeaks, finches, flickers, mockingbirds, mourning doves, and robins. Plant in full sun to partial shade, in well-drained average soil.

Rockspray cotoneaster (*Cotoneaster horizontalis*) is a trailing shrub that can be treated like a vine. It has shiny, bright red fruit. Attractive to blue jays, brown thrashers, cardinals, catbirds, cedar waxwings, robins, song sparrows, and wood thrushes. Plant in full sun to partial shade, in well-drained average to poor soil.

Virginia creeper (*Parthenocissus quinquefolia*) is a vine that is commonly seen along the edges of woods in the eastern U.S., with its clusters of small blue-black berries in late summer to fall. Attractive to bluebirds, bobwhites, brown thrashers, catbirds, chickadees, evening grosbeaks, flickers, bobwhites, house finches, mockingbirds, robins, scarlet tanagers, sparrows, tree swallows, tufted titmice, vireos, warblers, woodpeckers, and wood thrushes. Plant in full sun to partial shade, in any average soil.

Ground covers that offer birds food and shelter include Indian mock strawberry (*Duchesnea indica*) and wild or sand strawberry (*Fragaria chiloensis*), which form low mats and produce seed-filled fruit; bearberry (*Arctostaphylos uva-ursi*), a creeping shrub with persistent red berries; and lower-growing varieties of rosemary (*Rosmarius officinalis*), a rugged plant whose small flowers attract birds in winter and summer.

Wildflowers and Grasses

Many birds thrive on the seeds produced by the wildflowers and grasses that grow naturally in open fields, meadows, and prairies. In addition to native species, some garden flowers and ornamental grasses are also good seed sources for birds. Here are a few suggested perennials (plants having several-year-long life cycles) and annuals (plants having one-year life cycles).

Asters (*Aster* spp.) bear daisylike flowers of pink, purple, or white in summer to autumn. Plant in full sun, in moist but well-drained average to good soil. Perennial.

Bachelor's buttons (*Centaurea cyanus*) produce compact flower heads in blue, pink, rose, wine red, and white. Plant in full sun, in light, neutral soil. Annual.

Big bluestem (*Andropogon gerardii*) is a tall, clumping prairie grass that produces large, three-part purple spikes in summer. Plant in full sun, in average to good soil. Perennial.

Black-eyed Susans (*Rudbeckia* spp.) are golden daisy flowers with dark centers, and bloom for a long time in summer. Plant in full sun, in any average soil. Perennial.

Calendulas (*Calendula officinalis*) bear orange and bright yellow double, daisylike blooms in late fall through winter, or in spring. Plant in full sun, in well-drained average soil. Annual.

Coreopsis (*Coreopsis* spp.) yields a profusion of yellow, orange, maroon, or reddish flowers from late spring to fall. Plant in full sun, in any average soil. Perennial.

Fountain grass (*Pennisetum setaceum*) forms a dense, rounded clump of narrow, arching leaves. In summer, hollow stems are tipped with fuzzy, coppery pink or purplish flower spikes. Plant in full sun, in any soil; prefers a dry location. Annual.

Globe thistles (*Echinops* spp.) are small, cylindrical cactuses that bear long-tubed, many-petaled flowers in white, yellow, pink, and red. In warm climates, plant in full sun, in well-drained soil; in cool climates, plant in pots and bring inside during the winter months. Perennial.

Goldenrods (*Solidago* spp.) produce fluffy clusters of tiny golden flowers in late summer to fall. Plant in full sun, in average to poor soil. Perennial.

Indian grass (*Sorghastrum nutans*) is a tall, clumping prairie grass that produces loosely branched flower clusters with long golden hairs in summer. Plant in full sun or high shade, in average soil. Perennial.

Little bluestem (*Andropogon scoparius, Schizachyrium scoparium*) is an understory grass to big bluestem or Indian grass, and produces tiny seeds on orange stems through the winter. Plant in full sun to high shade, in average soil. Perennial.

Love-in-a-mist (*Nigella damascena*) produces solitary blue, white, or rose flowers on the ends of branches bearing thread-like leaves. They bloom quickly in the spring and dry up in the summer, producing papery-textured seed capsules. Plant in full sun or partial shade, in average soil. Annual.

Love-lies-bleeding (*Amaranthus caudatus*) is a grain-producing amaranth that bears red flowers in tassel-like clusters. Plant in full sun or partial shade, in average to poor soil. Annual.

Mexican sunflowers (*Tithonia rotundifolia*) have gaudy flower heads with orange-scarlet rays and tufted yellow centers. Plant in full sun, in average to poor soil. Annual.

Pincushion flowers (*Scabiosa caucasica*) produce flowers of blue, bluish lavender, and white with stamens that protrude beyond the surface of the flower cluster, giving the illusion of pins stuck in a cushion. Plant in full sun, in any average soil. Perennial.

Portulacas (*Portulaca grandiflora*) bear roselike flowers in brilliant shades of red, rose pink, orange, yellow, and white from early summer until frost. The flowers open fully only in sun and close in the late afternoon. Plant in full sun, in any soil, although sandy loam is preferable. Annual.

Purple coneflowers (*Echinacea purpurea*) have pinkish purple daisy flowers with drooping petals and orange to brown centers. Plant in full sun, in well-drained average to poor soil. Perennial.

Quaking grass (*Briza maxima*) produces clusters

of seed-bearing spikelets dangling from threadlike stems. Spikelets resemble rattlesnake rattles and are papery and straw-colored when dry. Plant in full sun, in average to poor soil. Annual.

Sunflowers (*Helianthus* spp.) have daisylike flowers, annual or perennial, of gold, orange, or white with large, dark centers, in summer. Plant in full sun, in moist but well-drained, fertile soil. Perennial.

Switchgrass (*Panicum virgatum*) is a tall, sometimes strikingly blue-stemmed clump grass. Plant in full sun, in average to poor soil with moderate to high moisture. Perennial.

Wild buckwheat (*Eriogonum* spp.) bears tiny blossoms in long-stemmed clusters that turn to shades of tan or rust as seeds ripen. Plant in full sun, in well-drained, loose, gravelly soil. Perennial.

Zinnias (*Zinnia elegans*) come in many strains with colorful, round flower heads in summer and early fall. Flower colors include white, pink, salmon, rose, red, yellow, orange, lavender, purple, and green. Plant in full sun, in good soil. Annual.

Other perennial seed sources for birds include bulbous oat grass (*Arrhenatherum elatius* var. *bulbosum*), scabiosa (*Scabiosa caucasica*), and tufted hair grass (*Deschampsia caespitosa*). Other good annuals include dandelion (*Taraxacum*), fountain grass (*Pennisetum setaceum*), and hare's tail grass (*Lagurus ovatus*).

Hummingbird Plants

Hummingbirds are drawn to tubular flowers in bright shades of red, orange, and pink. They poke their bills into the blossoms to sip the nectar and extract tiny insects, and pollinate the flowers in the process. Here are some hummingbird flower options.

American or wild columbine (*Aquilegia canadensis*) is a perennial growing to 2 feet high. Yellow flowers with tubular red spurs appear in late spring to early summer. Plant in full sun or filtered shade, in average soil.

Bee balm (*Monarda didyma*) is a perennial growing to about 3 feet high. Plants bear clusters of tubular flowers in shades of red, pink, purple, and white in summer. Plant in full sun or light afternoon shade, in average soil.

Cardinal flower (*Lobelia cardinalis*) is a perennial growing to 4 feet high. Its loose clusters of brilliant scarlet flowers in late summer contrast stikingly with the dark green, lance-shaped, toothed leaves. Plant in full sun or partial shade, in rich soil with constant moisture.

Coralbells (*Heuchera sanguinea, H. x brizoides*) are perennials growing to 2½ feet tall. Its clusters of small red, pink, or white bell-shaped flowers are carried atop tall, slender stems in spring and summer. Plant in full sun or light shade, in average soil.

Cypress vine (*Ipomoea quamoclit*) is a tender annual vine. It produces tubular scarlet flowers from early summer to early fall. Plant in full sun, in average to poor soil. Tolerates drought.

Fire pink (*Silene virginica*) is a short-lived perennial that can reach 2 feet in height. It has clusters of red flowers in spring and summer; the petals have toothed edges. Plant in full sun to partial shade, in average, well-drained, sandy or loamy soil.

Fuchsia (*Fuchsia* x *hybrida*) is a tender perennial grown as an annual except in frost-free climates. Plants bear drooping, bell-shaped flowers in various colors; choose red for hummingbirds. Plant in partial shade in a very moist location with rich soil.

Penstemon (*Penstemon barbatus*, *P. campanulatus* 'Garnet', *P. gloxinioides* 'Firebird') is a perennial that grows to 3 feet high. It produces spikes of tubular red flowers in spring or summer. *P. campanulatus* and *P. gloxinioides* are for warm climates only. Plant in full sun or light shade, in well-drained, loose soil.

Scarlet sage (*Salvia splendens*) is a tender perennial usually grown as an annual. Plants can reach 3 or more feet high where the growing season is long and warm. Plants have dark green leaves and bear upright spikes of tiny flowers with brilliant scarlet bracts (that look like petals) all summer until frost. Plant in full sun or partial shade, in any soil.

Texas sage (*Salvia coccinea*) is a tender perennial that grows to more than 2 feet high in warm climates. It bears spikes of scarlet flowers in spring and summer. Plant in full sun or partial shade, in any soil.

Other good plants for hummingbirds include lupines (*Lupinus* spp.), jewelweed (*Impatiens* spp.), red buckeye (*Aesculus Pavia*), scarlet paintbrush (*Crassula falcata*), snapdragons (*Antirrhinum* spp.), trumpet creeper (*Campsis radicans*), and trumpet honeysuckle (*Lonicera sempervirens*).

Birdfeeding

Although a bird population's principal source of nourishment will virtually always be local food plants—including those you may have put in yourself—there is also always a place for bird feeders in the landscape. Birds eat a tremendous amount of food for their size; the meaning we give to the phrase "eat like a bird" does not reflect the facts of the natural world. And because birds eat so much, even a lush environment can only support a limited number.

But adding a few feeders to supplement the available natural food sources will enable you to attract and sustain more birds than the neighborhood plants alone could feed. Indeed, installing a well-stocked feeder or two is one of the most reliable ways of attracting birds to your yard, even if you choose to do little else.

People tend to think of winter as the time bird feeders are needed, because plants are dormant and snow and severe weather make it more difficult for birds to track down food from natural sources. In summer, when natural foods are more abundant, it is easier for birds to find food for themselves. But while it is true that feeders are especially valuable in winter, year-round feeding will attract an even larger bird population to your property. It will also get the birds accustomed to a reliable source of food.

There are other advantages to summer feeding, too. You will see quite a few birds in summer that you don't see in winter.

The summer residents migrate up from their winter homes farther south. And the birds that are in residence throughout the year are often at their most colorful during the summer breeding season. Goldfinches are a good example; the males are a golden yellow in summer, but a more subdued grayish olive in winter.

Supplying plenty of food in spring may also encourage more birds to build nests and raise young in the area over the summer.

If you do decide to limit your birdfeeding activities to the winter, it is best to begin in late summer, or at least by early autumn. Fall migrations will be under way at this time, and species passing through the area will stop to eat. Some of them may decide to stay, instead of continuing farther south. Birds migrating into your area from farther north choose their winter territories in autumn, and they look for places where there's plenty to eat. If your feeders are stocked, more of them are likely to decide that your property would make a good winter home.

To find out which seeds your local birds like best, make a shallow wooden pan divided into several compartments and put a different kind of seed in each one. Once a day, write down the proportions of each kind of seed that is eaten. After a couple of weeks a definite pattern will emerge. Adjust your seed mix accordingly, putting in the greatest quantity of the kind of seed your birds eat most. Or skew the mix to attract precisely the birds you desire.

Bird Foods

To most effectively attract birds to the feeders in your yard, base your feeding program on suet (hard animal fat) and mixtures of different seeds and grains. You can also put out fruit, nuts, peanut butter, baked goods, and even insects. Hummingbirds prefer a special sugar syrup. Some foods can be offered year-round, and others are seasonal.

Suet provides birds with a quick energy source and helps them to maintain their high body temperatures (112°F). You can purchase it from a butcher shop and some supermarkets. The best suet comes from beef kidneys. Suet is a winter food; it quickly turns rancid when the temperature goes above 70°F.

Other fats, such as bacon fat and meat drippings, can be substituted for suet, as long as the fat does not contain a lot of seasonings. Birds will also eat American cheese or cream cheese. Other sources of fat and protein include finely minced or ground raw meat, canned dog food, and dry dog food crumbled or crushed and mixed with a little water.

Seeds of various sorts are enjoyed by many birds. You can buy commercial seed mixes (although the inexpensive ones often contain a lot of filler seeds that don't appeal to birds). Or purchase bags of individual seeds and make your own mixes, which often works out to be cheaper in the long run.

Seeds birds like include black oil sunflower seed, black-striped and gray-striped sunflower seeds, hulled sunflower seed, several types of millet (the best being white proso millet and red proso millet), Niger (thistle) seed, safflower seed, and canary seed. A mix with a high proportion of sunflower seeds or white proso millet is always a good bet, because they appeal to lots of birds. You can also add grains to the mix.

Put out seeds year-round. But bear in mind that hulled and cracked seeds will turn moldy if they get wet and remain wet. Keep the seeds dry if you can, or empty feeders after rain and refill with fresh seed.

Grains such as oats, buckwheat, and other kinds of wheat are fine feeder fillers. Cracked corn is a favorite food of quite a few birds; but when buying it, make sure the corn is cracked, not ground. Cracked corn and other cracked grains will spoil if they get wet, so keep them dry or clean feeders regularly. You can mix grains with seeds to serve in tray feeders at any time of year. Cornmeal can be mixed with suet or peanut butter, but it should not be added to seed mixes.

Fruit, in fresh, frozen, or dried form, is adored by numerous birds. Orioles and tanagers (as well as mockingbirds and starlings) especially go for it. In addition to those produced by plants in your garden, birds relish apples (raw or cooked), apricots, blueberries, cherries, currants, dates, crabapples, prunes, grapes, raisins, peaches, pears, strawberries, and watermelon (the seeds of which cardinals love).

Chop fruit into tiny pieces and put it in tray feeders, or nail half of an apple or orange, or a large piece of banana, to a feeding platform and let the birds peck at it. You can also break open a fresh coconut with a hammer and set out pieces of coconut still attached to the shell. Fruit is a summer food; it freezes in winter.

Nuts, including peanuts, pecans, and walnuts, are popular with birds. Some birds like peanuts in the shell, while others prefer peanut kernels. With pecans and walnuts, either remove them from the shells and chop them into small pieces, or split the shells in half and let the birds have them "on the half-shell." Squirrels also love nuts, and may beat the birds to them unless you squirrel-proof the feeders (see pages 50–52). Nuts are expensive, though, and are best as occasional treats, in any season.

Peanut butter is a good source of protein and fat, and is enjoyed by lots of birds, particularly juncos and chickadees, who seem to like it even better then suet. Mix peanut butter with seeds, corn meal, pan drippings, water, or other foods for easier eating.

Baked goods are not the most nutritious of foods, but birds are suckers for them. Birds will happily help you get rid of stale bread, leftover cake, pancakes, pie crust, or doughnuts. Crumble them up and spread them on a tray feeder. Baked goods spoil quickly in summer and are best served when the weather is cooler.

Insects and worms are expensive and should be considered a special treat. But if you really want to spoil the insect lovers among them, you can go to a fishing tackle store that sells bait and buy them crickets or worms. Or better yet, pick up mealworms (beetle grubs) at a pet shop. Birds that like insects or worms will also go for bits of bacon, cheese, or dry dog food.

Sugar syrup, prepared at home and served in a special feeder (see page 45), is a nice supplement to hummingbirds' normal diet of nectar and insects. To make sugar syrup, combine 1 part sugar with 4 parts water. Bring to a boil and boil just long enough to dissolve the sugar. Remove from heat, let cool, and pour into feeders. Quantities of sugar and water needed will depend on the size of your feeder, but it is important to maintain the 4-to-1 ratio. More can harm hummingbirds. It is not necessary (or advisable) to add red food coloring.

Grit is used by birds to grind up seed and other hard foods in their gizzards. (Birds have no teeth.) This essential digestive aid is hard to come by in winter when the ground is covered with snow and ice, and you'll be doing the birds a favor by supplying a ready source. Put out a shallow pan of crushed eggshells, coarse sand, or crushed charcoal (use filtering charcoal, not barbecue briquettes, which are chemically treated). Or you can buy poultry grit at a feed store if you live in a rural area. You can present the grit separately or add it to a seed mix at a rate of about a teaspoon of grit per quart of seed.

At Christmastime you can treat wild birds to their own tree. Decorate an outdoor evergreen with balls made of peanut butter, seeds, and grit; suet, seeds, and grit; or bits of fruit, shelled nuts, and suet. You can also hang strings of cranberries and popcorn on the branches (use a beading needle and thin fishing line to string them).

Favorite Foods

Although birds will eat a variety of different foods from the feeders in your yard, certain birds do show a decided preference for particular foods. If you wish, you can stock your feeders selectively to appeal to the birds you like best and, to some degree, discourage others. Here are the favorite foods of some common birds.

Blue jays: peanuts (in shell), peanut kernels, cracked corn, black oil sunflower seed, black- and gray-striped sunflower seeds, suet, fruit
Brown thrashers: fruit, cracked corn
Cardinal: sunflower seeds, fruit, safflower seeds, suet
Catbirds: fruit
Cedar waxwings: fruit
Chickadees: sunflower seeds, suet, peanut butter, peanut kernels, safflower seeds
Cowbirds: cracked corn, white proso millet
Juncos: white proso millet, peanut butter, hulled sunflower seeds, cracked corn, Niger seed-suet mixtures
Evening grosbeaks: sunflower seeds, nuts, cracked corn
Finches, house: Niger seed, hulled sunflower seeds, white proso millet, fruit, flax seed, red proso millet, canary seed
Finches, purple: sunflower seeds (except gray-striped), Niger seed, fruit, canary seed
Flickers: black- and gray-striped sunflower seed, suet
Goldfinches: Niger seed, sunflower seeds, fruit
Grackles: sunflower seeds, millet, cracked corn, oats, peanut hearts, peanut kernels
Mockingbirds: fruit, suet, peanut butter mixtures, mealworms

Mourning doves: cracked corn, millet, black oil sunflower seed, canary seed, Niger seed

Northern orioles: fruit, suet

Nuthatches, red-breasted: black- and gray-striped sunflower seeds, fruit

Nuthatches, white-breasted: black- and gray-striped sunflower seeds, black oil sunflower seeds, suet

Pine siskins: black oil sunflower seed, hulled sunflower seeds

Phoebe: fruit

Red-winged blackbirds: cracked corn, millet

Robins: fruit, cracked corn, mealworms

Rufous-sided towhees: cracked corn, millet

Scrub jays: black- and gray-striped sunflower seeds, black oil sunflower seed, suet, peanut kernels

Sparrows, chipping: cracked corn, suet

Sparrows, fox: black- and gray-striped sunflower seeds, white proso millet

Sparrows, song: suet, cracked corn, millet, canary seed, Niger seed

Sparrows, tree: cracked corn, white proso millet, red proso millet

Sparrows, white-crowned: cracked corn, white proso millet, peanut hearts

Sparrows, white-throated: cracked corn, peanut kernels, millet, hulled sunflower seed, safflower seed

Tanagers: fruit

Tufted titmice: black- and gray-striped sunflower seeds, black oil sunflower seed, peanut kernels, fruit, suet

Woodpeckers, downy: suet, black- and gray-striped sunflower seeds, fruit

Woodpeckers, hairy: suet, black- and gray-striped sunflower seeds, fruit

Woodpeckers, red-bellied: suet, fruit, cracked corn, sunflower seeds

Wood thrushes: fruit

Special Treats

If you want to do something particularly nice for your birds, here are recipes for some simple tasty snacks they'll love.

Peanut butter alfresco

Mix together equal parts of peanut butter and cornmeal, and spread on a rough-barked tree branch.

Suet cakes two ways

In these recipes, the suet is melted twice because it becomes harder after the second melting.

1. Mix ½ cup ground dry dog food or dog biscuits, ½ cup sunflower seeds or seed mix, 1 tablespoon peanut butter, and ¼ cup raisins or finely chopped apple in a pie pan until well blended. Melt 1 cup suet in the top of a double boiler. Remove from heat and let cool until solid. Melt again, then pour over mixture in pie pan. Refrigerate until solid. Serve in the pan or cut into pieces and place in tray or suet feeders.

2. Mix 1 cup sunflower seeds and 1 cup cornmeal. Melt 1 cup suet, let cool until solid, then melt again. Add ½ cup peanut butter and stir until blended. Pour over dry ingredients and mix thoroughly. Pour into pans or harden partially and pack into suet feeders. Refrigerate until hardened.

Stuffed pine cones three ways

Attach florist's wire or string to pine cones for hanging before you stuff them with any of these three mixes. These mixes can also be served in log feeders.

1. Mix equal parts of sunflower seeds and red or white proso millet. Roll or dip a pine cone in melted suet to coat it. Roll the pine cone in the seed mixture, pressing as you roll, and let harden. Repeat the procedure for a thicker coating. To use in a log feeder, mix the ingredients together and stuff into the holes in the feeder when partially hardened.

2. Melt suet or meat fat. Stir in sunflower seeds, seed mix, or cornmeal until the mixture has a pasty or doughy consistency. Stuff into pine cones, packing it in between the scales. You can also spread this mixture on a tree branch.

3. Mix peanut butter and melted suet with raisins, peanut kernels or other chopped nuts, and black oil sunflower seeds. Stuff the mixture into pine cones or a log feeder.

Feeders

Bird feeders can be designed in a whole range of styles, each suited to dispensing a different kind of food for birds—such as suet, seeds, or sugar syrup for hummingbirds. A feeder can be as simple as a board with thin strips of wood nailed around the edges to hold the food. You can make your own feeders or buy them from garden centers, wildlife conservation groups, or shops that sell birding supplies.

Hopper feeders consist of a bin to hold seed and grains and a small tray attached to the bottom to dispense it. Some have an overhang to keep the tray dry. As birds empty the tray it is automatically refilled from the hopper. Hopper feeders may be hung, mounted on poles, or attached to windowsills.

Tube feeders are generally made of plastic and have holes of various sizes in the sides with perches for small birds to sit and peck Niger and sunflower seeds (millet is not recommended). Some tube feeders have a tray attached to the base to catch any spillover. Tube feeders are usually suspended from trees. If squirrels are a problem in your garden, you may want to install a baffle to keep them (see pages 50–52) from the feeder; and try removing the perches to discourage pesky, large birds, which can quickly empty a tube feeder.

Window feeders, of the hopper or platform type, are a treat for birdwatchers of all ages. Feeders installed at first-floor windows draw the most birds, although house finches, house sparrows, and some other birds will go higher. Close the blinds or lower the shade inside the window until birds get used to the feeder. Or you can buy window feeders with one-way glass backs that allow you to look out without the birds seeing in. Keep the feeder filled with fresh food, even though it may take at least a week or two until the birds begin to visit regularly.

Platform and tray feeders are shallow pans that are used to distribute nuts, fruit, suet mixes, seeds, and grains. They may be set on short legs near ground level or they mounted on poles. You can also make use of flat spaces already available on your property for mounting platform feeders. Retaining walls, tree stumps, and fence posts are all possible sites.

Suet feeders come into their own in winter, when they dispense suet, and mixtures of suet, peanut butter, seeds, and other foods. Suet feeders must allow the birds access to peck at the food. Mounting suet feeders directly on a tree can lead to severe trunk damage, so it is preferable to mount them on a board which is then attached to the tree, mount them directly on a dead tree or against a pole, or hang them.

Cage feeders made of mesh or netting and featuring open tops are the simplest suet feeders. Though common, plastic netting can be easily torn by crows, hawks, vultures, and racoons, and is very brittle in cold weather. A plastic-coated wire mesh is the best option. You can also make a cage feeder from a plastic berry basket, or simply fill a mesh bag and hang it on a tree trunk. Cage feeders can also be filled with nutmeats.

Bin feeders are simple wooden hoppers with hinged lids. They can hold suet if the front of the feeder is made with a plastic mesh panel.

Log feeders can be constructed with a length of branch about 18 inches long and 4 inches in diameter. Attach a screw eye to one end from which to hang the log, then cut or drill several holes 1 to 1½ inches in diameter partway into the sides of the log. It is unnecessary to install perches, which mainly have the effect of making the feeder more accessible to pesky starlings. Pack a suet or peanut butter mix into the holes and hang the feeder from a tree branch.

Hummingbird feeders, which dispense sugar syrup, are available in various sizes and shapes. If hummingbirds are not common in your area, a small 2-ounce feeder will probably be sufficient. If your garden attracts lots of hummingbirds, you will need one or more large-capacity feeders. Look for durable plastic construction, with red accents somewhere on the feeder to lure the birds.

Besides these structures, you can also use pine cones, into which suet and peanut butter mixes have been stuffed, as well as coconut shells, grapefruit and orange half-shells, and clean cat food and tuna cans filled with suet or suet mixes as feeders.

Feeders in the Garden

Just as different birds have a special liking for particular kinds of foods, they prefer different types of feeders, too. Some birds like a perch to wrap their feet around while they eat, others like to sit on a platform above the ground, and others feel most comfortable close to the ground. Of course, there are also quite a few that aren't picky.

Ground feeders attract blackbirds, brown thrashers, cardinals, finches, flickers, goldfinches, grackles, grosbeaks, jays, juncos, mockingbirds, mourning doves, robins, sparrows, towhees, and thrushes.

Platform and tray feeders on posts attract brown thrashers, chickadees, finches, flickers, goldfinches, grackles, grosbeaks, jays, juncos, mockingbirds, nuthatches, orioles, pine siskins, sparrows, tanagers, titmice, thrushes, warblers, and wrens.

Hanging feeders attract chickadees, finches, goldfinches, orioles, pine siskins, sparrows, tanagers, titmice, warblers, and woodpeckers (downy, hairy, and red-bellied).

Suet feeders attract chickadees, chipping sparrows, flickers, grackles, jays, mockingbirds, nuthatches, red-shouldered hawks, starlings, titmice, and woodpeckers.

Unless you wish to attract only selected birds, it's a good idea to use a variety of feeders with different food offerings. An ideal assortment of feeders would include one or more platform or tray feeders at ground level, some platform feeders atop 5- to 8-foot-high posts, several hopper and tube feeders suspended

5 to 8 feet above the ground, and a number of suet feeders attached to tree trunks at several different heights.

If your property is large enough, set up two or more feeding stations, each with an assortment of feeders, in different areas. If your yard is small and you have space for only one feeder, make it a platform feeder on top of a post, to attract the greatest variety of birds.

Place feeders between 4 and 20 feet from sources of cover—near groups of shrubs and trees, or at the edge of a woods, but not so near that a hungry cat would have a convenient spot for pouncing. For winter feeding, try to find a location that is sheltered from the prevailing wind—to the south of an evergreen hedge, wall, or the house, for example.

If you want to have a feeder near the house for a close look at your visitors, you may need to lead birds there gradually. Start with a feeder placed where birds feel comfortable and move it closer to the house by a few feet each week or so; the birds will follow. Eventually you will be able to feed them right outside a window where you can sit and watch them. They will get used to your presence and movements inside the house.

If you want birds to visit a window feeder, try this method starting with a pole-mounted feeder. Or rig up a clothesline on a pulley between the windowsill and a tree some distance away. Hang from the clothesline a feeder similar to the one in the window, and pull it closer to the window gradually over a couple of weeks. Birds will grow increasingly comfortable feeding near the house and will soon be using the window feeder.

Feeder Care and Maintenance

Bird feeders need regular cleaning. Uneaten food will spoil, either rotting or turning moldy. Bird droppings, feathers, stray insects, shells, and other debris can collect in the bottoms of feeders. Salmonella bacteria and other disease organisms can grow in spoiled food and may infect or even kill birds that ingest them.

Shells, husks, chaff, and droppings can cover the ground underneath feeders, too, and can eventually kill the lawn grass growing there. To preserve the lawn, it's a good idea to change the positions of your feeders by a foot or two every year. Return the feeder to its original spot after a hiatus of a couple of years. Or you can simply locate the feeders over areas where there is no turf growing.

How often you clean your feeders and what you clean them with will depend upon what the feeders are made of. The easiest feeders to clean are those made of plastic, glass, ceramic, or metal. Once a month, wash them in hot, sudsy water to which you have also added a little liquid chlorine bleach (about a tablespoonful per gallon of water). Skip the bleach when washing wooden feeders so you don't lighten the wood. Instead, use an antibacterial kitchen soap. Rinse thoroughly with clear water after washing, to eliminate any soap residue.

The monthly cleaning schedule is generally fine for tube, hopper, tray, platform, and suet feeders. In rainy, warm weather, however, you may need to wash out feeders more often.

Hummingbird feeders need to be cleaned every few days, or at least once a week. Sugar water ferments quickly in summer, and black mold may form inside the feeder. If no mold has formed on the feeder or in the syrup, simply empty the old syrup and rinse the feeder thoroughly with clear, warm water. If mold has developed, empty the feeder and discard the syrup, then add a mixture of warm water and vinegar. Shake well. To loosen mold from the sides of the feeder, add some raw rice or barley to the vinegar water and shake the feeder vigorously. If you are unable to loosen all the mold that way, use a stiff-bristled toothbrush or bottle brush to scrape it off. When the feeder is clean and all traces of mold are gone, rinse thoroughly with clear, warm water. Refill with fresh syrup.

If you have been feeding birds on the ground, you need to take care to maintain the area. As with feeders, spoiled food, bird droppings, and other debris can accumulate on the ground and create an unsanitary situation that might be dangerous to birds. Periodically rake up and discard the material in the feeding area to ensure healthy conditions for ground-feeding visitors.

Bullies, Pests, and Predators

Besides the birds you want in your backyard, feeders attract a host of other visitors, and not all of them are welcome. Squirrels can be a major annoyance, as can greedy birds like starlings and blue jays. Chipmunks, mice, and rats may also be drawn to feeders. And birds may face attacks from predators, most often cats and occasionally hawks or owls.

European starlings are among the most irritating of birds, stuffing themselves at feeders and pushing other birds out of the way. Try filling feeders with foods they don't like. Starlings dislike sunflower and safflower seeds (they are drawn by dog food, table scraps, and millet). To keep them out of suet feeders, make the feeders with three solid sides and a mesh bottom. Starlings can't hang upside down to eat, but woodpeckers and nuthatches can. You may also want to give preference to tubular over hopper or tray feeders, where starlings are particularly active. Finally, put out food in the early morning and late afternoon to avoid the the starlings' peak feeding time, which is around midday.

Squirrels are entertaining, and they're ingenious at getting into bird feeders.

They will leap surprising distances, slither down wires, and twist themselves into seemingly impossible positions to get into the birds' pantry. And once they get in, they can empty it in short order. Then they might chew on the feeder, too. When squirrels take over they scare the birds away.

If you don't mind squirrels, put out extra food for them. Try luring them away from the bird feeders by providing some of their own favorite foods in a different location; nuts, dry corn (on or off the cob), stale bread, and fruit may draw them.

To keep squirrels away from feeders, make sure the feeders are at least 5 feet above the ground and 8 to 10 feet away from trees, overhanging branches, or buildings—out of squirrels' leaping range. One way to accomplish this is to tie fishing line to a sinker and hurl it over a high branch, far out from the tree trunk, and then attach the feeder. The feeder appears to be suspended in midair, and the line is too long for squirrels to be able to climb down it.

A smooth plastic dome (or baffle) above a tube feeder may keep the squirrels away. You can also string several pie pans on the wires from which a feeder hangs, or install a wide, flat sheet of metal on the supporting pole under a feeder. A metal collar shaped like a funnel and placed on the pole 4 feet or more above the ground is another possibility. Metal poles are better squirrel deterrents than wooden poles; also, metal poles can be greased, and that will make them even more effective. Tube feeders wrapped with plastic-coated wire mesh keep squirrels away from the seeds although they can still get to the feeder. If all else fails, buy a squirrel-proof feeder with a weight-sensitive cover that snaps shut under a squirrel's weight.

Chipmunks, mice, and rats are attracted by spilled seeds. Don't spread food directly on the ground, rig up trays under feeders to catch spills, and don't use mixed seeds, which are especially attractive to them.

Cats threaten adult birds and also youngsters in nests. Belled collars may help to warn birds when cats are nearby. Put feeders high above the ground and at least 4 feet (but no more than 15 feet) away from shrubs and other places cats could hide. Use metal poles or wood poles sheathed in metal for pole feeders to discourage cats from climbing up. Prune overhanging branches where cats could perch and jump down onto birds. Finally, if at all possible, keep your cats indoors, both day and night; cats are most effective hunters after dark.

Hawks and owls sometimes hunt near backyard bird feeders, usually in winter when prey is scarce in the less-populated areas they prefer. There is, unfortunately, little you can do to protect birds from them. But hawks are scared off easily and seldom stay in populated areas for long (though some species are becoming more and more common in urban and suburban areas). If a hawk is persistent, you can put up a temporary brush pile and scatter seed inside it so the birds can eat under cover until the hawk becomes discouraged and moves on. Owls hunt at night—when other birds are not active—and anyway do not attack birds often.

Sometimes, even the birds you've invited can be rather pesky guests. Some birds, unfortunately, enjoy munching on young plants and will happily uproot seedlings of corn, beans, peas, and other edibles and ornamentals to devour the tender buds, leaves, and shoots.

One way to keep the local avian population out of your vegetable garden is to cover emerging plants with "floating" covers of lightweight spun-bonded polyester (one popular type is sold under the brand name Reemay). These covers are readily available at garden centers. When the plants are several inches high and no longer so attractive to birds, you can remove the covers. Fine-mesh netting is also available to cover fruit trees you may want to protect from the birds and harvest for yourself.

Light, movement, and sound can also keep birds away from your tender crops. Try stringing glittering, whirling aluminum pie pans or dangling some tin cans on fishing line or clothesline above your garden plot. Your garden supply store may even carry inflatable bird-scare balloons decorated with giant "eyes" and reflective stickers. Silvery, flashing strips of Mylar plastic hung from the branches will also discourage some of these greedy birds.

Water Sources

In the wild, birds get the water they need from ponds, streams, puddles, dew, and, of course, snow and rain. In a small backyard there's often not a stream or pond, and not enough available dew or puddles to supply the needs of more than a few birds. Besides, a natural water source could dry up during a summer drought and freeze solid in winter. Supplying a reliable source of water will do as much to attract birds to your garden as feeders full of food.

Backyard water sources include birdbaths, pools, and small fountains. If you have a pool or pond in your yard, don't use any chemicals to treat the water. Avoid the use of chemical products to control insects or algae, or to keep the water from freezing. If you have garden plants growing in or near the water, don't use chemical fertilizers or pesticides on them. Be careful, too, to avoid runoff from gardens farther away. If your water source involves plumbing, do not use lead pipes; PVC is a better choice.

Any water source for birds should be shallow—at least around the edges—and have a bottom that slopes gradually. A rough surface around the edge is also important to allow birds to stand and drink without slipping. Concrete, stone, pebbles, or sand are all fine.

Locating the water source

When deciding where to put a water source for birds, consider first and foremost the birds' safety. Birds are particularly vulnerable to predators when they are wet. For most birds, the best location for water is out in the open, at least 4 feet away from shrubs, dense plantings, or overhanging tree branches where cats could hide. The birds will, however, appreciate a tree or some cover 10 to 15 feet away from the water. They will fly there to groom themselves after bathing, and can quickly reach safety when threatened. A stalking cat would be easily spotted crossing the open area.

If you have a woodland that attracts shy forest birds like wood thrushes, a more protected location for the water source is better. Put the water in the shelter of shrubs or a mixed hedgerow or dense border. For safety reasons, a birdbath raised on a pedestal is better than a ground-level pool in a sheltered area.

It's great fun to watch birds as they bathe—some take quick, demure dips and others splash around like children playing. So try to put a pool or birdbath near a deck, porch, patio, or bench, or where it is easily viewed from inside the house, so you can watch what goes on.

For convenience, a location near a faucet is recommended. If your water source requires electricity to operate a pump or heater, you will probably need to have an electrician run a line out to the garden. Don't rely on extension cords for more than occasional use.

Water in winter

One of the most important considerations in providing water for birds is keeping it unfrozen in winter. Birds need less water in winter than in summer because they don't use it for bathing, but they still need to drink. At a time when natural water sources in the neighborhood are likely to be frozen, it is vital that your water source remain clear of ice.

If you've got just a single birdbath or a very small pool, the easiest way to thaw it is simply to pour in a pan of boiling water once or twice a day. A better solution is to keep your water source from freezing at all, by installing an immersion heater intended for outdoor use. You can purchase an immersion heater from a mail-order garden supply company, a local garden center, or a hardware store.

The devices come in different sizes; use a small heater for a birdbath or tiny, shallow pool, and a larger heater for a bigger pool. Whichever size you buy, make sure it has an automatic thermostat that shuts it off when the water thaws.

If you live in a mild climate where you experience only occasional brief spells of freezing weather, you can forego the heater in favor of a simple heating tape.

Water in motion

Birds seem irresistibly drawn to dripping, bubbling, gently flowing water. A splashing fountain or trickling waterfall would be a delightful addition to the backyard bird garden. A fountain or waterfall should be shallow and have a gentle flow of water that will not frighten the birds away. You can buy kits for simple waterfalls or fountains at local garden centers and from water garden supply companies. Larger, more complicated designs will require professional installation.

There are simpler ways than a full-fledged fountain or waterfall to put water in motion in your garden. One method is to run a hose up a tree trunk and out along a low branch, with the nozzle pointing downward. Position a birdbath underneath the nozzle. Turn on the hose just enough to allow water to drip down into the birdbath. Or you can set the nozzle for a fine mist and turn on the hose a couple of times a day at regular times. Birds will learn the schedule and take turns flying through the spray. They also enjoy flying through sprinklers.

Birdbaths

A birdbath is the easiest, least expensive way to provide water for local birds. You can buy a birdbath or make your own, but either way there are several considerations to keep in mind no matter which kind you choose.

Birdbaths can be set directly on the ground or placed on pedestals. Ideally, you should have both kinds. Some birds prefer to drink at ground level, and a ground-level basin is especially welcome in an open area. A pedestal, on the other hand, is important where there is vegetation in the vicinity that could camouflage a predator. Pedestals are generally about 3 feet high, which will put the birdbath beyond the reach of most predators. Be warned, however, that determined cats can jump that high, so be watchful if you have cats that spend time outdoors.

Whatever kind of birdbath you choose, make sure it is at least 1 foot across (2 to 3 feet is better) and no more than 3 inches deep. Look for a rough surface on which birds can maintain a secure footing, and a bowl with a gentle angle from the edge to the deepest water in the center instead of a sharp drop.

Birdbaths can come in a variety of materials.

Concrete birdbaths are the most common. A rough surface which birds grasp easily with their feet, concrete also has enough weight to make the baths stable atop pedestals. These can crack, however, if left outside during the winter.

Clay and glazed ceramic birdbaths are usually suspended on chains or cords. They are attractive, but like concrete bird baths, ceramic baths can crack in cold weather, and are often too slippery for bathing.

Plastic birdbaths are lightweight and easy to move, but they tip over easily and the smooth surfaces are slippery for birds. You can roughen the surface with sandpaper, or by applying some no-slip bathtub decals. Or you can spread water-proof glue over the surface near the edges, then sprinkle with sand. (Wait until the glue is completely dry and brush away any loose sand before filling the bath.)

> Dust baths help birds condition their feathers and get rid of parasites on their skin and among their feathers. Give them an area of bare dirt or sand in addition to water for bathing.

Metal birdbaths, like plastic ones, are lightweight, and they also have smooth surfaces that should be modified for easier perching. If you opt for a metal birdbath, choose one made of stainless steel or painted with rust-resistant paint. And locate a metal bath in the shade—metal gets hot in the sun.

Wooden birdbaths are uncommon, and don't last as long as those made of other materials. If wood appeals to you, look for a bath with a plastic liner.

You can also make your own birdbaths from old trash can lids, recycled saucepans or baking pans, or plastic plant saucers. Clay plant saucers will work, too, if the bottoms are glazed.

Clean birdbaths every day or two in summer. Empty the birdbath, scrub it with a brush to remove any algae, rinse well, and refill with fresh water.

Small Pools

A step up from a ground-level birdbath is a small pool that, depending on its size, offers an opportunity to grow some aquatic plants and perhaps even accommodate some fish, frogs, or turtles in addition to providing water for birds. A pool can be as simple as a small, shallow basin, a birdbath minus the pedestal, or another container set into the ground. As with birdbaths, if the container surface is smooth, be sure to modify it so birds can find stable footing. And as with birdbaths, be sure to locate the pool between 4 and 15 feet away from cover.

To install the container, set it on the ground and trace its outline in the dirt with a stick or dowel. Dig a hole to the dimensions of the outline and deep enough so the rim of the container will project 2 inches above the ground level. This lip will prevent dirt from washing into the pool.

For a somewhat larger pool, you can purchase a flexible plastic liner or a preformed liner of fiberglass or plastic from a water garden supply company. Pool liners are available in a variety of sizes, and they come with instructions for installation. Liner pools can be installed in a day or a weekend, and preformed pools take even less time.

To install a liner pool, excavate to the necessary dimensions and depth, level the bottom, add a 1-inch layer of sand, and level that. Then set the liner in the hole, fill with water, and let it settle. The next day you cut off the excess from the flexible liner to leave a flap measuring up to 12 inches on all sides. Peg these flaps to the ground, and cover them with flagstones or flat rocks to hide them. You can plant waterlilies, lotuses, and other aquatic plants in containers to set on the bottom of the pool. You will probably also want to place some rocks in the pool near the edges for birds to use as platforms when drinking, but be careful to use rocks with smooth bottoms that will not tear the pool liner.

In a pool or pond with a steep rather than a gradual drop, place near the edge some flat-topped stones large enough so that their tops are above the water. The stones will provide a place for birds to perch and drink. Some birds don't like to stand on a flat surface, but instead need to grasp a support with their feet. For them, arrange a slender branch or a good-sized twig to extend out over the water just at the surface. In a larger, deeper pool or pond, the large, flat leaves of waterlilies and lotuses can provide a platform for little birds.

Homes for Birds

To backyard birders, there can be nothing more satisfying than having birds set up house in their yards. Not only does a nest mean a permanent tenant in the garden, but also, in due time, the delight of seeing baby birds raised right outside the door. It is also a nice affirmation that the landscape is especially inviting.

Manicured lawns that are meticulously kept over every square inch are not good material-hunting grounds for nest-building birds. They find more to work with in disheveled, unkempt areas where leaves and dead twigs are left on the ground and dry grasses lie about the edges of the lawn. It's a good excuse for the gardener to be a little lazy.

Just as they do when taking shelter from the elements or hungry predators, birds look principally to trees, shrubs, vines, and other plants as places to locate their homes and raise families. If the vegetation on your property is slight, the best way to encourage nesting is to provide more.

You can also build and set up nesting boxes (birdhouses) and nesting shelves. Nesting boxes and shelves can be quite effective in attracting a range of cavity-nesting birds. Particularly with the available cavity-nesting space rapidly diminishing—as forests are cleared for agriculture and development and homeowners regularly remove dead trees from their property—these boxes will be warmly welcomed.

But there are other means, as well, of attracting nesting birds to your yard. Whether you intend for the birds to make their nests amid your plantings or in nesting boxes, you can help them by putting out various nesting materials to supplement the natural materials—bits of bark, grass, thistle down, leaves, moss, feathers, mud, and small twigs—already available.

Some good materials to set out include: animal hair and fur, collected from brushes; cotton, from rolls, not balls; cloth, cut into thin strips; cellophane (wrappers), from food and household items, cut into thin strips; down, from old pillows, coats, or comforters; excelsior (used in packaging); human hair, collected from combs and brushes; pillow stuffing; rope, unraveled into strands; string; thread; wool; and yarn. (Any pieces of long, stringlike material should be no more than 4 to 6 inches in length, or the birds could get tangled up in them.)

Put out nesting materials in early spring (around the time when you see the first robins). It doesn't matter if the weather is still cold, or even if the ground is still frozen or covered with snow. Some birds start building nests early in the season, and will look elsewhere if you don't make materials readily available.

Scatter nesting materials about the property where birds are likely to notice them, and make them easy to spot. Put an assortment of nesting materials in a couple of baskets hung from tree branches, or stuff them into suet feeders that are not filled with suet. You can also mount an open box in a prominent place, filled with nest ingredients. Stringy material can be draped over shrubs and hung on clotheslines as well.

Nesting Boxes

You can buy nesting boxes or build your own from a kit or from scratch. But whether you plan to buy or build, there are certain considerations you should keep in mind.

Select a nesting box to attract a particular species of bird. Different birds prefer boxes of different dimensions, with entry holes of particular sizes and at particular heights above the floor. Some birds (such as phoebes, robins, and barn swallows) prefer nesting shelves—boxes with one or more open sides.

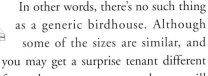

In other words, there's no such thing as a generic birdhouse. Although some of the sizes are similar, and you may get a surprise tenant different from the one you expected, you will have the best chance of success if you put up boxes that are the right size for birds you often see on your property.

Construct nesting boxes to the dimensions given for individual birds on pages 70–71, or buy a kit at a garden center or hardware store, or through a mail-order supplier. Experienced do-it-yourselfers can build boxes from plans found in any number of books on home woodworking or attracting birds.

Whatever size birdhouse you select, make it a single-unit

dwelling. Purple martins are happy in apartment-type houses, but other birds like places of their own. Unless your goal is to attract purple martins, each nest box should accommodate just one family of birds.

Birds like simple designs best. You can buy all sorts of adorable fancy birdhouses designed to look like Victorian houses or thatched-roof cottages, for equally fancy prices. These bird-houses make cute garden ornaments, but they just might not attract any tenants. A simple box with a round opening for a front door is a better choice. If you can't resist buying one of the more elaborate models, at least make sure it has no moving parts, which would surely frighten away any prospective tenants.

Build nesting boxes of a material that is durable, weather-resistant, and "breathable" so air can get in and moisture will not accumulate inside. The best material is wood that is well-seasoned so it will not split or warp, and that is $3/4$ to 1 inch thick. Treat the wood with a nontoxic wood preservative or paint it before putting the box together. Or simply use a weather- and rot-resistant wood such as redwood, cedar, or cypress. Neutral browns, greens, and grays are good colors for nesting boxes. White is a good choice for a house in a sunny location—it won't hold as much heat inside as a darker color.

Do not use plastic for a nesting box; because it is not porous moisture can build up inside to unhealthy levels. Avoid metal, too, because a metal house would get too hot inside and the young could die.

Construct the nesting box with brass or galvanized hardware that will not rust. Hinge the top or one side and fasten with a small latch hook so you can easily open the box for cleaning.

It is not necessary to install a perch at the entrance to a nesting box. Although they will use it, birds don't need the perch. And there's also a risk that squirrels or cats or house sparrows will be attracted by it.

Drill a few small holes along the top of each side of the box for ventilation. This will help ensure that nestlings don't overheat during hot spells. For protection from rain, you can give the roof a sufficient pitch to shed water and add a strip of metal or roofing paper to the ridge to make it waterproof. If the roof is level, you can cover it with roofing paper or paint it heavily; cutting a groove across the underside of the overhanging part will prevent water from draining back into the interior.

A nesting box will last longer in cold-weather climates if its sides extend below the bottom of the box. This drains off water that otherwise might freeze in the cracks between the bottom and the

sides and force them apart. You can also drill small holes in the bottom of the box to drain water that may have gotten inside.

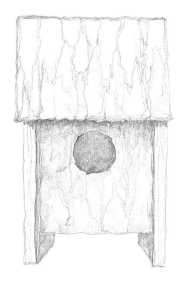

Nesting Boxes in the Garden

It is a good idea to put up nesting boxes in late summer or early fall for use the following year. Installing them before the trees lose their leaves will enable you to choose a location that will not be too densely shaded. A place in partial to light shade is generally best; woodland birds, however, prefer more shade. Most birds tend to avoid boxes put up in dense woods.

Mount nesting boxes securely, nailing them firmly to a tree or post. Nailing a box to a tree generally will not harm the tree, provided it measures at least 8 inches in diameter. Avoid attaching the box with a wire encircling the tree, which can damage and eventually kill it.

Think about where and how you will mount a nesting box before you build it. Mount it with the entrance facing away from prevailing winds. The entrance must be level or angled slightly downward so rain will not collect inside. When mounting the box on a tree trunk, attach a strip of wood to the back of the box near the top and bottom. This will prevent it from resting against the tree, where it could soak up moisture during rainy weather.

If you have enough space, put up several houses of different sizes on your property. Since birds are territorial, it is unlikely that you will get more than one nesting pair of any given species. The houses should be spaced far enough apart so that nesting birds won't feel their territory is threatened; otherwise, you may end up with none of the boxes being occupied.

You can use most of the same strategies to safeguard nesting boxes that you use to keep predators away from bird feeders (see pages 50–52). Boxes mounted on poles can be protected with smooth plastic or metal squirrel guards and metal collars.

To keep cats from climbing a tree trunk to reach a nesting box, one effective (but not especially aesthetic) method is to wrap the trunk with a piece of sheet metal 1½ to 2 feet wide. The metal collar should fit snugly around the tree, but not so tightly that it cuts into the bark. Install the metal collar about 5 feet above the ground. Tree trunks grow, so check periodically to make sure the metal band is not constricting growth.

Clean out nesting boxes after the baby birds have left the nest for good. Old nesting materials seem to harbor parasites that could infect the next brood of nestlings. And in any case, most birds will not want to build in a box where there's already an old nest. You can clean out the old nest material either in fall or early spring.

Dead or dying trees are useful to cavity-nesting birds, who make their homes in the holes. If you have one, and it is in an unused corner of the property where it would do no harm if it fell in a storm, consider allowing it to stand as a potential nesting site. Tall tree stumps, too, can house cavity nesters.

If any of the sides of the boxes are cracked or rotted, this is a good time to replace them. You can also spray the inside with insecticidal soap to kill any hidden insects.

Nesting Box Specifications

Cavity-nesting birds are very particular about the specifications of the nesting boxes and nesting shelves in which they're willing to make their homes. The box itself must be of a specific size, and entry holes must be a particular size and distance from the floor of the box. Here are the dimensions, installation heights, and recommended locations for nesting boxes and shelves for a variety of common birds.

Bluebirds, eastern, mountain, or western: 5" wide x 5" deep x 8–12" high. Hole 1½" in diameter and 6–10" above floor. Locate 4–6' above ground, in open field or meadow, or along forest edge.

Chickadees (various species): 4" wide x 4" deep x 8–10" high. Hole 1⅛" in diameter and 6–8" above floor. Locate 4–15' above ground, along forest edge, in woodsy area, or where there are lots of trees.

Finches, house: 6" wide x 6" deep x 6" high. Hole 2½" in diameter and 4" above floor. Locate 6–20' above ground, in trees, shrubs, vines, or open areas.

Flickers, common: 7" wide x 7" deep x 16–18" high. Hole 2½" in diameter and 14–16" above floor. Locate 6–20' above ground, near forest edge or in open places.

Flycatchers, great crested: 6" wide x 6" deep x 8–12" high. Hole 1¾" in diameter and 6–10" above floor. Locate 5–15' above ground, in woods.

Nuthatches, red-breasted, pygmy, brown-headed, or white-breasted: 4" wide x 4" deep x 8–10" high. Hole 1¼" in diameter (1⅜" for white-breasted) and 6–8" above floor. Locate 5–15' above ground, along forest edge, or in mixed woodland.

Purple martins: 6" wide x 6" deep x 6" high. Hole 2¼" in diameter and 1–2" above floor. Single or multi-unit houses. Locate 6–20' above ground, in open area near water.

Phoebes: 6" x 6" shelf, open on one or more sides. Locate 8–12' above ground, under porch or roof.

Robins: 6" x 8" shelf , open on one or more sides. Locate 6–15' above ground, in tree, next to building, near edge of woods, in grove of trees, or in mixed border next to lawn.

Swallows, barn: 6" x 6" shelf, open on all sides. Locate 8–12' above ground, in barn or open building 6" from roof.

Swallows, tree or violet-green: 5" wide x 5" deep x 6–8" high. Hole 1½ in diameter and 4" above floor. Locate 5–15' above ground, in open area near water.

Titmice: 4" wide x 4" deep x 10–12" high. Hole 1¼" in diameter and 6–10" above floor. Locate 5–15' above ground, along forest edge or in open area.

Warblers, prothonotary: 5" wide x 5" deep x 6" high. Hole 1⅛" in diameter and 4–5" from floor. Locate 4–8' above ground, in leafy glade or dappled shade near pond or stream.

Woodpeckers, downy: 4" wide x 4" deep x 8–10" high. Hole 1 ¼" in diameter and 6–8" above floor. Locate 5–15' above ground, in woods.

Woodpeckers, hairy or golden-fronted: 6" wide x 6" deep x 12–15" high. Hole 1½ in diameter (2" for golden-fronted) and 9–12" above floor. Locate 8–20' above ground, in woods.

Woodpeckers, red-bellied or red-headed: 6" wide x 6" deep x 12–15" high. Hole 2 1/2" in diameter (2" for red-headed) and 9–12" above floor. Locate 12–20' above ground, in edge of woods or field.

Wrens, Bewick's or house: 4" wide x 4" deep x 6–8" high. Hole 1¼" in diameter and 4–6" above floor. Locate 5–10' above ground, in open woods or edge of woods.

Enjoying Backyard Birds

Along with the satisfaction of providing food, water, and shelter for wild birds comes the fun of watching them. Birds are endlessly fascinating creatures and will provide you with hours of entertainment as they conduct their daily activities. The more time you spend watching birds, the more you will learn about them. You can learn to identify the species that visit your property, and you'll get glimpses into the surprisingly complex lives of these little creatures. Their behavior may surprise you in many ways when you come to understand what it means. You may also come to appreciate the uniqueness of the various songs and calls of your feathered visitors.

To get started watching birds, you will want to get yourself a pair of field glasses or binoculars (see pages 86–87) and a good field guide to help with identification (see page 90).

When you're watching birds, it's important that they do not see you. You will probably do a lot of your backyard birdwatching from inside the house, through windows with good views of feeders, nesting boxes, birdbaths, and plants that birds like to use for food or shelter. You might want to set up an observation post at the most-used window, with a couple of chairs and a small table where you can keep binoculars handy. (If you are keeping a birding journal, store it here with your other supplies.) Outdoors, a bench in a quiet corner, or a deck or patio are other good places from which to observe birds.

Whenever you are watching birds, try to position yourself

where the birds are not likely to notice you. Hold as still as you can, especially if they can see you; sharp movements and noise will frighten them. When scanning with binoculars or switching your attention from one bird to another, try to make slow, smooth movements.

You'll soon learn to recognize the most frequent visitors to your backyard. With careful observation, you'll discover the different ways in which birds feed and the foods they prefer. Their styles of bathing and their courtship behavior will become familiar. You may also have the thrill of watching birds build nests, lay eggs, and feed their nestlings. You'll find out how they vocalize to defend territory, warn of danger, attract mates, and locate their young.

Recording these details in a journal can help you see patterns over time (see pages 88–89). But even if you don't write down what you see, the time you devote to watching the birds you've helped attract to your backyard will be time well spent.

Identifying Birds

As you become familiar with the birds that visit your feeders and make use of plants and water sources you have provided for them, you will learn to tell them apart. Inevitably you will want to know which birds are visiting you. You will soon find that you see certain kinds of birds only during the summer or during the winter, and others all year round. You will also find that different birds show up for a week or a few weeks in spring or fall. These species are migrating through your area on their way to their summer or winter homes. Certain birds may pass through every year. And you may also have an occasional surprise visitor that you see just once, or only very rarely.

A good field guide is essential to identifying birds accurately (see page 90 for some recommendations). Most field guides are organized by families of birds, and you will find yourself paging through the book over and over, searching for a bird you've seen. As you learn more about birds, you will be able to tell some of the families apart, which will make identification easier. You'll be able to recognize, for example, that the bird at your feeder is likely to be some sort of sparrow or wren or warbler.

To make good use of a field guide, keep it handy and take note of the following characteristics when you see the bird:

• the size and shape of the body
• the shape and position of the wings, at rest and in flight
• the color of the wings, back, and head
• the color or pattern on the breast (Many sparrows, for

example, have breasts streaked with brown, but a dark spot on the breast helps identify a sparrow as a song sparrow.)

- the shape and position of the tail (Chimney swifts, for example, have short, stubby tails; swallows have forked or notched tails; and wrens hold their tails up.)
- the size and shape of the beak
- unique features of the head (Does it have a crest? Are there any markings around the eyes or on the head or neck?)
- the silhouette of the bird in flight, and its flight pattern
- marks on the wings that become evident in flight (Mockingbirds, for examples, have white wing bars that you can see when they fly.)

Also look for differences between males and females. The two sexes look very similar in some species and quite different in others. Breeding pairs often feed together, and you may be able to identify females by the males they are with.

Birds may look different at different times of year. Some birds, primarily males, take on brighter coloring during the spring and summer mating season.

Bird Behavior

Ethology is the name given to the scientific study of behavior. Ethologists study birds and other animals to find out why they do certain things, and whether all the members of a species, family, or other biological unit share the same behavioral traits. Watching the birds in your backyard will reveal to you many aspects of their behavior. You may even find, over time, that some of the behaviors you see are so interesting that you want to keep notes of your observations.

In the meantime, you can spend many enjoyable hours learning about the behavior of the birds that visit your property. Observe how birds act when they eat, bathe, court prospective mates, defend their territories, and feed their young. You can watch them as they build nests and care for babies, how they groom themselves, and how they interact with members of their species and with birds of other species. There's a lot to see.

Feeding

Once you've provided different kinds of feeders and natural food sources, you will have an excellent opportunity to study the different ways birds act when they eat. Watch how different birds approach feeders. Do they come one at a time or in groups? Which birds dominate the feeder and chase other birds away? Which ones will share? Notice how the more aggressive birds frighten off the shyer ones. You may find that a flock includes one dominant bird who chases the others away if they get too close when it is eating. Watch for the bird to scare off other species and members of its own group by running toward them, head down, as if to peck at them.

It's interesting to watch how different birds take their food, too. Chickadees will fly to a feeder, take one sunflower seed, and fly to a nearby branch to open the seed and eat the kernel. House finches sometimes sit right down in the feeder and eat one seed after another; titmice do the same, if they can crack the seeds open. Blue jays stuff their mouths and fly away. Some birds carry on so much at the feeder that they spill the seed all over the ground.

Watch your birds as they make use of natural food sources, too. You will see them pull berries from stems, pick insects from shoots and twigs or (like swifts and swallows) catch them in midair, probe for food in the ground or (like woodpeckers and nuthatches) under the bark of a tree, and forage in leaf litter. Rufous-sided towhees, for example, are fun to watch as they dig through dead leaves under shrubs or at the edge of a woods looking for food. They jump and push backward with both feet while simultaneously propelling their bodies forward, in the process stirring up the leaves. Then they poke around with their bills. In this sort of goofy way they work their way along under the bushes.

After eating, many birds like to wipe their bills on a branch, first on one side, then the other.

Bathing and grooming

Watch how different birds bathe. Some perch on the edge of the birdbath, take a drink, then suddenly dip their heads and throw water over their backs. Others jump right in and splash around until they're soaking wet. Some birds prefer to fly through a sprinkler, and do so over and over on a hot afternoon.

After bathing, birds will fly to a nearby branch to preen themselves. They take one feather at a time and run it through

their bills to smoothe it. Many birds also oil their feathers, much as we might put on body lotion after a bath. They spread oil onto their feathers from a gland located near the base of the tail.

Some birds like to take dust baths, either instead of or

78

in addition to water baths. House sparrows, especially, love dusting, and make it a social occasion. They often gather in dusty spots in big, noisy groups to flutter and dip in the dirt. You may see birds sitting on top of an ant nest and letting the ants climb all over them. Scientists aren't sure why birds do this, but some believe it is a grooming behavior. One theory is that the ants release formic acid, which may kill parasites on the birds' feathers or skin.

Courtship

Birds engage in courtship behavior to stimulate mating and egg-laying. Courtship behavior can be very simple or amazingly complicated, and it varies greatly from one species to another. In fact, courtship behavior allows males and females to identify one another as members of the same species. Often a male in pursuit of a female will chase away other males of the same species, and then chase after the female. A male cardinal woos a female by offering her bits of food. A male song sparrow takes a more direct approach, flying into a female in midair to get her attention. Mourning doves gently touch bills, as if they were kissing.

Bird pairs stay together for varying lengths of time. Swans

mate for life. House wrens, on the other hand, mate for just one brood. After the eggs hatch the female takes off to find another mate to produce a second brood. The male stays behind to feed the nestlings.

Nesting

In some species males and females work together to build a nest. In others one or the other gender does the work. A male house wren chooses a site (often a nesting box) and carries twigs, dry grass, and other materials to it to build the nest. He may build nests in more than one place to improve his chances. When he attracts a female to the nest she inspects his work. If it suits her she will add soft down and other material to line the nest. If she's not happy with the nest she may take it all apart and rebuild it until it pleases her.

While the eggs are incubating the parents turn the eggs

several times each day. When the nestlings hatch, the parents regularly clean the nest, getting rid of eggshells and carrying off the droppings of the babies.

Those youngsters must be fed, too, and they squawk noisily for the parents to feed them. The parent whose job it is to feed the nestlings shuttles back and forth all day between the nest and the preferred hunting grounds, returning time after time with grubs or insects for the young.

Even after the youngsters are out of the nest they may try to get their parents to feed them. You may see a young bird, especially a ground-feeding species, trailing around after one or the other parent, begging to be fed. The baby crouches down with its mouth open, crying and fluttering its wings. Often the par-

ent will stoically ignore the wailing youngster as long as it can, then will break down and give it a morsel of food.

Sometimes you may see a family group that just doesn't look right—the baby is too big for the parents. In that case the parents are probably raising an adopted child. Cowbirds, in particular, are known for dropping their eggs into the nests of other birds, in effect farming out the babies to be reared by someone else. You will see the exhausted-looking foster parents trying to satisfy a wailing lummox of a baby that is bigger than either of them and reluctant to start fending for itself.

Defending territory

Before building a nest or attracting a mate, the male bird establishes his territory. If you watch the birds in your yard closely, you will probably be able to discern the boundaries of some of the territories. The most obvious display of territorial behavior is put on by male robins in spring. When you see male robins spread out over a lawn, each of them is establishing his territory. Males of the same species jockey for position, and then defend their territory against interlopers. Defense may take the form of aggressive behavior or songs, and it goes on throughout the mating and nesting season.

A male red-winged blackbird defends his territory by flying from perch to perch around the borders, emitting a sharp three-syllable song.

Sometimes two male birds will face off on the ground. The threatening bird opens its bill as if to bite, lowers its head, and spreads its wings. The retreating bird lowers its bill, hunches its shoulders, and turns away from the aggressor.

In some species the gender roles are reversed. Among hummingbirds, it's the females who claim territories, build nests, and find mates.

When a predator enters the territory, defensive behavior becomes extreme. A male mockingbird, for example, will dive-bomb local cats, flying straight at their heads and dancing in the air in front of them, if they come close to a nest when crossing the yard. The cats are likely to ignore the repeated attacks.

A male house wren will try to lure predators away from the nest by flying in front of them to attract their attention and get them to follow him.

Often birds will work together to chase off a predator or threat. It's not unusual to see a group of blackbirds or other smaller birds flying around a crow to force it out of the territory. Even birds of different species may cooperate to drive away a common predator.

Songs and Calls

Birds vocalize in different ways, and the sounds they make often have particular meanings. Most birds make more than one kind of sound. Blue jays, for example, are best known for their loud, raspy calls. But they also have a beautiful clear, bell-like call. You can learn to recognize some of the different sounds made by birds that are common to your garden, and you may also be able to figure out what they mean.

Experts in bird behavior believe birds use different calls and songs for a variety of reasons: to defend their territories from other males, to warn of danger (such as a lurking predator), to locate their youngsters, and to attract a mate. They also use calls to convey information about food, especially during migration.

Calls are short sounds that are not musical. Red-winged blackbirds have a very distinctive territorial call—a rather harsh, three-syllable cry that sounds like "konk-la-ree" or "honk-a-ree." The red-breasted nuthatch calls with a high, nasal "yank-yank-yank" reminiscent of the tooting of a tin horn, while the white-breasted nuthatch utters a low "yank" or "yair."

The melodious bird sounds are called songs and are sung exclusively by males. Birds make sounds throughout the year, but they only sing when they are mating and nesting in spring and summer. In early spring you begin to hear bits of song from different birds, as if the males are warming up. When the females come to town the males burst forth in song, presenting their entire repertoire.

Bird songs differ widely among species, and there are even differences among members of the same species. Song sparrows, for example, all sing different songs, and each bird may have over a dozen distinct numbers. In effect, song sparrows also use their songs to identify themselves as individuals—presenting their calling cards, so to speak.

Probably the most curious of singers is the mockingbird. Mockingbirds are accomplished mimics who are known for imitating the songs of other birds. If you hear, in rapid succession, snatches of cardinal, robin, red-winged blackbird, blue jay, tufted titmouse, and oriole, all coming from the same place, it's a mockingbird. Mockingbirds are often active at night, so in addition to the songs of other daytime birds you may also hear them mimicking the trilling of spring peepers or katydids. Mockingbirds have their own songs, too. They don't always "mock." No one has yet been able to figure out just why mockingbirds copy the songs of other birds.

Listening to the sounds of birds can be addictive, and you will probably find, as you get to know your local birds by sight, that you will want to learn to pick out their songs and calls from the neighborhood chorus.

A good way to get started is to buy any one of the various collections of recordings of different birds. These give the name of a bird, followed by its most characteristic songs and calls, often with several variations. You can find them at shops selling birdwatching and nature-related materials, and advertised in birding magazines (see page 90).

Equipment

Field glasses or binoculars (or, for the more advanced, a spotting scope or small telescope) will give you a closer look at birds, making it easier to identify them and observe them as they go about their activities.

Field glasses are made of two parallel tubes, each of which contains a sliding inner tube. Lenses are attached to each tube. Field glasses are relatively inexpensive and provide 5- to 6-times (5x to 6x) magnification. They are not strong enough for birdwatching in the wild, but are perfectly adequate for most backyard situations.

Binoculars are recommended if your property is large and wooded, or if you expect to expand your birdwatching activities beyond the backyard. They are similar to field glasses, but the tubes contain prisms that reflect light along the tubes and make possible greater degrees of magnification. Generally, the higher the power of magnification, the larger and heavier (and more expensive) the binoculars. A 6x to 10x magnification is fine for most birders. It is rather difficult to hold higher-powered binoculars steady.

As magnification increases, the field of view narrows, and you will need to practice using the binoculars to become adept at locating birds in trees and keeping them in view when they move. Wide-angle binoculars that afford a wider field of view are especially good for beginners.

Buy binoculars from a reputable store that will allow you to try them out before you buy them. Take them outdoors to test them. Look for glasses that are coated with magnesium fluoride on the lenses and prisms. They should be marked "fully coated" and should be an even violet or amber color. Make sure the mechanical parts of the glasses operate smoothly and are not loose or wobbly.

Spend the money to buy a decent pair of glasses manufactured by a good company; cheap glasses will not perform as well and may give you eyestrain or headaches. Examine the glasses for scratches on the lenses before you buy them. Choose the lightest pair that meets all the above criteria. And make sure you get a warranty.

Spotting scopes and telescopes, along with a tripod, are valuable if you plan to spend a lot of time watching birds out in the field, perhaps planning trips and vacations around birdwatching activities. Scopes are especially useful for birdwatching over the ocean or other large bodies of water. Look for a scope with a 20x magnification, or a 10x to 15x magnification with a zoom lens that can give a 20x magnification. Choose a scope and tripod that are easy to carry and set up quickly.

Spotting scopes and telescopes are not cheap, but if you're going to get one, invest in a good one. A cheap scope will not give you sharp, clear images, and just won't hold up as well under use. And an inexpensive, flimsy tripod won't hold a scope steady in strong winds.

Clean field glasses, binoculars, and scopes regularly with lens tissue or a soft artist's paintbrush.

Keeping a Journal

Keeping a journal of your birdwatching makes the experience richer and can also become a great educational tool. You'll be surprised at how much you will learn about birds just by keeping records of what you see.

To prevent journal keeping from becoming too time-consuming, you may want to keep regular records of a few birds that are particularly interesting to you, and sporadic notes on unusual or striking occurrences involving other birds.

You can buy journals and diaries especially designed for birdwatchers (these are often full of interesting tidbits of bird-related information). But a loose-leaf or spiral-bound notebook or a hardcover blank book will serve just as well.

If you are artistically inclined and think you might want to try sketching some of the birds you see, buy a spiral-bound artist's drawing pad and use it as a combination sketchbook and journal. Keep your journal in a convenient place so you will write in it regularly.

Keep a running log of birds you see around your property, where you see them, and what they are doing. Note their favorite foods (both natural and supplemental), water sources, and cover plants, and use this information to modify your bird garden season after season.

If you can, try to make daily notations. Jot down weather conditions, too. You may find that you spot some unusual birds just after a major storm.

Your notes on what birds are doing may lead you to closer observations of the behavior of your favorite birds. This is the best way to learn to identify what certain behaviors mean. You may even discover a new trait you haven't read about in books or heard about from other enthusiasts.

You may wish to keep records on the arrival and departure of seasonal residents and migrant species. After a few years of noting dates you will know almost to the day when to expect them to return to your garden.

When the mating and nesting season arrives, you can keep records on which of the nesting materials you supplied were most popular, and, if you can track them, which birds used which materials. Note the locations of any nests you can find. If you can peek into the nest *without touching it*, count how many eggs it contains. And watch what the parents do to chase you away. Later on, note how many babies are hatched, how many are successfully fledged, and how long it takes.

If you go on birdwatching trips, you can add these experiences to your journal, too, noting where you went and when, and what you saw.

To make it easier to find notes on particular birds when you page through your journal, underline their names.

Keep your journals from year to year, and make it a point to look through them from time to time. You will see patterns of behavior emerging, as well as arrival and departure schedules, eating habits, and mating seasons. Your journals will make your birdwatching all the more enjoyable.

Resources for Birders

Books

Bull, John. John Farrand, Jr., ed. Rev. by Lori Hogan. *The National Audubon Society Field Guide to North American Birds: Eastern Region.* New York: Alfred A. Knopf, 1994.

Coe, James. *Eastern Birds.* New York: Golden Books, 1994.

Peterson, Roger Tory. *Eastern Birds,* 4th ed. Boston: Houghton Mifflin, 1980.

—. *Western Birds,* 3rd ed. Boston: Houghton Mifflin, 1990.

Robbins, Chandler S., Bertel Bruun, and Herbert S. Zim. *Birds of North America.* New York: Golden Press, 1983.

Stokes, Donald W., and Lillian Stokes. *A Guide to Bird Behavior.* 3 volumes. Boston: Little, Brown, 1979, 1983, 1989.

Tufts, Craig, and Peter Loewer. *The National Wildlife Federation's Guide to Gardening for Wildlife.* Emmaus, Pa.: Rodale Press, 1995.

Udvardy, Miklos D.F. John Farrand, Jr., ed. Rev. by Lori Hogan. *The National Audubon Society Field Guide to North American Birds: Western Region.* New York: Alfred A. Knopf, 1994.

Available from the U.S. Fish and Wildlife Service, 1849 C St., NW, Washington, DC 20240: *Backyard Bird Feeding, Backyard Bird Problems, Homes for Birds, Migratory Songbird Conservation.*

Magazines and periodicals

Audubon Field Notes, published by the National Audubon Society

Birding, published by the American Birding Association

Birding News Survey, Avian Publications, Inc., P.O.Box 310, Elizabethtown, KY 42701

Birder's World, 44 E. 8th St., Suite 410, Holland, MI 49423

Bird Watcher's Digest, P.O. Box 110, Marietta, OH 45750

Wild Bird Magazine, Box 6050, Mission Viejo, CA 92690

Recordings

Walton, Richard K., and Robert W. Lawson. Roger Tory Peterson, ed. *Peterson Field Guide to Backyard Bird Song*. Boston: Houghton Mifflin, 1991 (cassette), 1994 (compact disc).

—. *Birding by Ear: Eastern and Central North America*. Boston: Houghton Mifflin, 1989 (cassette), 1994 (compact disc).

—. *Birding by Ear: Western*. Boston: Houghton Mifflin, 1990 (cassette), 1994 (compact disc).

Groups and organizations

American Backyard Bird Society, P.O. Box 10046, Rockville, MD 20849

American Birding Association, P.O. Box 6599, Colorado Springs, CO 80934

American Bird Conservancy, 1250 24th St., NW, Suite 500, Washington, DC 20037

Conservation International, 1015 18th St., NW, Suite 1000, Washington, DC 20036

Cornell Laboratory of Ornithology, 159 Sapsucker Woods Rd., Ithaca, NY 14850

Defenders of Wildlife, 1101 14th St., NW, Suite 1400, Washington, DC 20005

National Audubon Society, Membership Data Center, P.O. Box 51003, Boulder, CO 80323

National Fish & Wildlife Foundation, 18th and C. Sts., NW, Suite 2556, Washington, DC 20240

National Wildlife Federation, Backyard Wildlife Habitat Program, 1400 16th St., NW, Washington, DC 20036

The Nature Conservancy, 1815 North Lynn St., Arlington, VA 22209

Wildlife Conservation Society, International Wildlife Conservation Park, 180 5th St. and Southern Blvd., Bronx, NY 10460

World Wildlife Fund, 1250 25th St., NW, Washington, DC 20037

Index

Iridescent hummingbirds, bright red cardinals, and sprightly chickadees are just a few of the many visitors you can attract to your own backyard. Learn how to provide a safe haven for migrating  birds. Find out what the essential elements are to attract wildlife to your yard or garden. The National Wildlife Federation's Backyard Wildlife Habitat™ program can teach you how to create and maintain your own patch of the natural world. The NWF provides the necessary tools to get you started and even offers official Backyard Wildlife Habitat™ certification. Join the more than 17,000 certified participants across the country!

The mission of the National Wildlife Federation is to educate, inspire, and assist individuals and organizations of diverse cultures to conserve wildlife and other natural resources and to protect the Earth's environment in order to achieve a peaceful, equitable, and sustainable future.

For information on the NWF's Backyard Wildlife Habitat™ program or how to become a member of the National Wildlife Federation, please write to: National Wildlife Federation, 8925 Leesburg Pike, Vienna, VA 22184-0001.